Analyze this!
A Risk Management Analysis Program

Bob Kruijsse

DEDICATION

I dedicate this book to all those who are interested in the practical use of Risk
Management Analysis and who are willing to start
Rethinking Risk Financing.

CONTENTS

ACKNOWLEDGMENTS

First I would like to thank my father Joseph Marien Kruijsse, who was one of The Netherlands first experts in computers (when a computer still took up half a building) and thanks to whom I have a penchant for logical and analytical thinking.

I also would like to thank all those people who have been involved in my educational process in Risk and Insurance Management, which started in 1980 and continues on a daily basis until today. My first "teacher" in insurance was a seasoned insurance broker from Rotterdam, L.E.M. Kaptein, who taught me all the logical bases for insurance. Also, all the customers I have served as an insurance broker and insurance company and the work I did as a Risk and Insurance Manager, have taught me how to look at different businesses through the same glasses.

Last but certainly not least I would like to thank my wife Elzbieta for having the patience with me during those times that life was more riskfull than I would have wanted it to be...

1 RISKS AND FORESEEABILITY

Risk is something we all have to handle from day to day. Whether you walk down the street, drive a car, ride a horse or go up in an elevator. All these things have some inherent risks in them and we are all expected to handle them on a continuing basis.

Now let's have a look at what risk is about. What is Risk, indeed. Some people see it as danger, others think risk is fun!! An insurance company may see its customers as the main risk. Now we can go into a further multitude of discussions and definitions, but for me it is still simply the uncertain event which awaits you and which has a negative effect on your financial status. RISK represents UNCERTAINTY. The more uncertainty there is in an activity the greater the difficult in managing towards a successful completion.

However, an event would need to be UNCERTAIN and have a SIGNIFICANT impact.

Although many definitions of Risk exist, one that I see as most logical is that risk is the uncertainty regarding the occurrence of a loss or other business adversity which has or will have negative (financial) results for the risk taker.

I would not go into the direction of seeing Risk as synonymous with Loss. A Risk can be a loss, but it can also give you a gain. A game in a casino has risk in it, but you may win money.

Looking at risk, or better said, at the risks you expect to get "thrown at your feet" will help you avoid surprises. Especially the unpleasant ones. It will help you exploit the opportunities you may find en route. It will make you feel better.

But, here comes the question "What can we expect, or better said, what can we foresee?" Clearly not everything, as is clearly shown from these comments, made by people who perhaps later regretted them:

"The 'telephone' has too many shortcomings to be seriously considered a means of communication."
Western Union Internal Memo, 1876

"Who the hell wants to hear actors talk?"
Harry M. Warner, Warner Bros, 1927

"There is no reason for any individuals to have a computer in their home."
Ken Olsen, President, Chairman and Founder of DEC, 1977

"Heavier-than-air flying machines are impossible."
Lord Kelvin, President, Royal Society 1895

"Airplanes are interesting toys but of no military value."
Marshall Ferdinand Foch, Professor of Strategy, Ecole Superiure de Guerre

As you see, these are perhaps not risks perse, but still show you how difficult it is to foresee what is going to happen.

Even more clearly, in an interview in 1907 a newspaper stated that:

"When anyone asks me how I can best describe my experience in nearly 40 years at sea, I merely say- uneventful. Of course there have been winter storms and gales and fog and the like, but in all my experience I have never been in an accident of any sort worth speaking about. I have seen but one vessel in distress in all my years at sea- a brig, the crew of which was taken off in a small boat in charge of my third officer. I never saw a wreck and have never

wrecked, nor was I ever in any predicament that threatened to end in disaster of any sort. "
Reference: *"Disaster At Last Befalls Capt. Smith,"* New York *Times, April 16, 1912.*

This, at that time still not famous, Mr. Smith had his last job as Captain of a large oceangoing passenger vessel. This was…..the Titanic.

Now how deep do we see risks? As you know, car accidents happen, but the repair of the car is just one part of your financial loss; the time lost in handling everything, your health…. We can go on and on; that is why I see every risk being just the tip of the iceberg. There is that well-known picture of an iceberg showing that more than 70% of it is underwater!

Or, as the dictionary says on Markov:

'A sequence of events, the probability for each of which is the dependent on the event immediately preceding it.'_

But, to say it simple, one follows the other – consequences always exist, whatever you do.

2 RISKS AND WHAT DO WE DO WITH THEM

What kinds of Risk Management do we see nowadays: Many. That is clear; many names, and even more specialized kinds. Some of these are in the business/enterprise/hazard and others are clear pure financial risks.

Army	*Flood*
Audit	*Governance*
Banking	*Hazard*
Basel II	*Hedging*
Business	*Hospital*
Commodities	*Insurance*
Country	*Investment*
Credit	*Market*
Crisis	*Operational*
Disaster	*Project*
Enterprise	*Solvency II*

All of these have the addendum Risk Management after it, but are in reality completely different kind of disciplines. Yes, they look at risks, but do so from different perspectives and with different needs in mind.

I myself am more specialized in Insurance Risk Management; with some Enterprise and Hazard risk management mixed in. But for example Flood Risk Management is a very specific natural risk, which again has its own specialists. Also not mentioned here in this list is Contract Risk Management, which has aspects of legal knowledge, as contracts are always legal documents.

This brings us to the next thing: We must do something with the risks. That is clear; we should remove them, control them; shortly said; we should manage the risks, so that they have a lesser influence on that what we (plan) to do. We must get knowledge of the risks; and in order to be able to do so, we must remove the ignorance.
Risk has always been there even at the dawn of history. Moses wrote nearly 3500 years ago: "Every new house must have a guard rail around the edge of the flat rooftop to prevent anyone from falling of". This was clearly Risk Management.

As with many management disciplines, risk management is too frequently relegated to an academic exercise. Many organizations do an excellent job of the initial steps of identifying and qualifying risks on paper, but fail to develop and apply the findings of this analysis to deliver against the bottom line. These organizations squander a real opportunity to leverage the knowledge gained to validate initial plans, progress towards improved efficiency, and drive better business decisions.

Risk management must become an integral component of an organization's management processes and, as said before, many corporations in Europe are not yet fully aware of the extent and breadth of their catastrophic exposure. It is therefore imperative that corporate customers closely cooperate with their insurance and risk advisors.

Most people still look at insurance being *the* solution to risk. But let's not forget, that every insurance cover has holes in it. It is more important to decide what to do with the risk.

The next logical step is not only to consider not only how to spend less in traditional protection, such as insurance, but also how to spend this money better to protect the corporation against those risks, which really touch the well-being of said organization.

Of course, some business risks might be very difficult to insure, such as health and ecological liabilities, patents infringements, consumer boycotts strikes, internal mistakes etc.

Normal Day-to-Day occurrences are handled by the basic Management Controls, every organization (should have) has in place. The risk events foreseen in the Risk Management Analysis and listed in the Risk Register are handled by the Risk Management System in place. Only the unforeseen risks (and they *do* occur), should be tried to stop by Crisis Management.

Crisis Management may be a follow-up, but also a standard procedure, once a huge unexpected risk shows itself. But using this instead of RM, means that each and every occurrence provides to that situation. Than we really have something we could even call Risky Management, which can be seen as making decisions that are not based on a careful consideration of the facts.

The graphs on the next page show the difference between using the normal Management Controls in combination with Risk Management vs. just the Crisis Management.

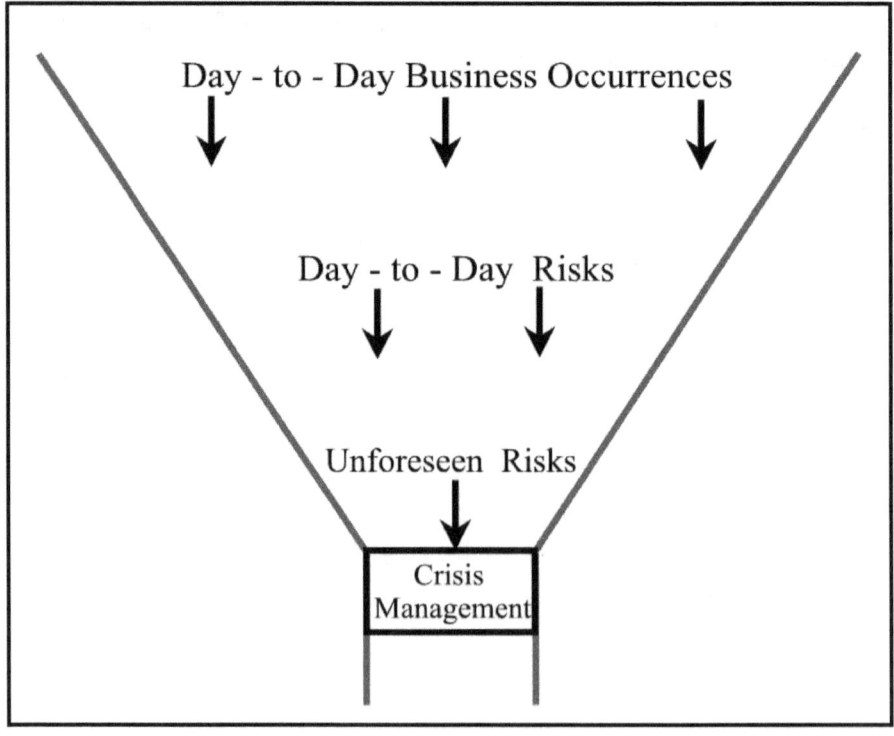

The organization, its staff, management and shareholders are better protected by having a working Risk Management system in place.

Risk Management versus Insurance

As stated before, the traditional method of handling risk has been to arrange for it to be transferred – i.e. to insurance.

However, in recent years risk management has started to take a much higher profile particularly in the public sector and major corporations. In my view this should be taken as a very positive move as the traditional insurance risk transfer route is fundamentally flawed for the following reasons:

1.   Insurance does not cover all risks.
2.   Even where insurance does cover the loss, there is often major business disruption which is not met by insurance.
3.   If risk is not managed there will be a high incidence of claims which leads to high premiums therefore reduced profitability and possibly uninsurability.

Risk transfer towards insurance should be treated as an action of last resort.

In order to achieve this benefit it is necessary to have an effective risk management program in place, which continually seeks to identify, assess and control areas of risk exposure.

The scale of savings to be gained from effective risk management should not be underestimated and is certainly not restricted to the direct or visible costs such as compensation payment, equipment replacement etc for which insurance is often held. Detailed studies have shown that for every €1 of 'insured' loss (or loss covered by the loss fund) between €8 - €36 of 'invisible' loss is also incurred.

The normal risk management procedure is as follows –

1. Identification of risk.
    2. Evaluation of risk.

3. Removal of risk.
    4. Reduction of risk.
        5. Retention of risk
            6. Transfer of risk.

Risk identification is the process, which allows for a possible future problem to be recorded in a database. The information must be sufficiently detailed to allow a normal assessment of the risk, thus supporting subsequent management decisions. Many organizations think that once this process is done, risk management itself has been done – and when the risk management process is continued, will an organization realize its risk management investment.

New risks will be recognized during the course of the program by those working within their own areas of responsibility. Risks will also be exposed at reviews and meetings.

Once a risk has been identified, we have to **Evaluate the risk** and estimate the probability of a risk occurring, and the potential impact of the risk on the program. Only then can resources by used for the most important issues.

Now we see if it is possible to **Remove** the risk. This is the most simple solution in Risk Management. Once a risk has been removed, we no longer need to worry or do anything about it. This is also called Risk Avoidance. Eliminating a loss exposure by ceasing or never undertaking an activity that produces the exposure. In making this decision, the person or organization must weigh the potential value of the activity against the potential loss. We also remove the risk by educating the employees of an organization. Education and knowledge of what may happen will reduce significantly the number of "at risk moments" and "almost occurrences". Through this, we have a much lower number of occurrences, where assistance is required.

But, if we cannot fully remove the risk, perhaps it is possible to **Reduce the risk.** Lowering the possibility of a risk occurring, lowers the possibility of a negative impact on our balance sheet.

Risks which have not been removed and have just been reduced or not, we keep, as one of the major tools is **Risk Retention** wherever possible. This is the planned assumption of risk by an insured through deductibles, policy retentions, or self-insurance. The reason for a risk retention is usually to reduce expenses and improve cash flow, to increase control of claims reserving and claims settlements, or to fund losses that cannot be insured. But please do not forget that retention is dangerous. It must be offset against the probability of a major risk occurring.

At this moment we will start to mitigate our risks and this will reduce the number of losses (uninsured losses have the trend to be assigned to their culprits) and will produce direct and immediate cost savings, but a good risk management program is required to make it work.

Transfer of risk can have different possibilities. The traditional transfer method used is insurance, but also contractual transference falls under this group. As I already said in the previous chapter, risk transfer towards insurance should be treated as an action of last resort. Noninsurance Transfer is a risk management technique for shifting an organization's potential losses to others. Many alternatives are available that may be less costly than insurance, such as subcontracting part of a project or inserting a hold-harmless agreement in a contract.

Once these actions have been taken, we should check the results:

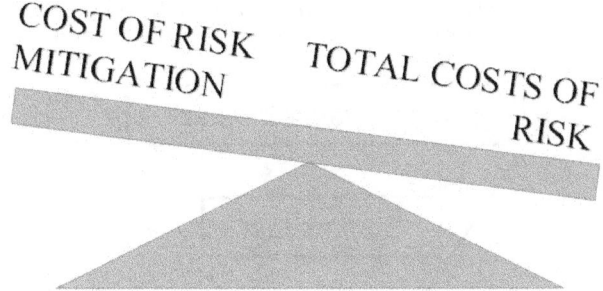

No, this is not meant to be in balance!! The Total Costs of Risk should always come out to be lower that the costs of mitigation. *(see chapter 4)*

In order to be able to check this result, we look at the costs of risk retention (or if you want look at any other risk handling system, where the same idea applies) and see that the costs of this risk handling method should always be lower than the Total Costs of Risk. *(see chapter 4)*

So if we now compare the graphs on page 8 with the one below, we see that all our risk mitigation methods should lead to eliminate as many of the at risk moments as possible. This will lead to a much lesser number of occurrences when assistance is needed (and these occurrences are already costing money). Once an occurrence becomes a claim, there will be real time lost and the costs of such an occurrence increases. Every occurrence has hidden costs as explained in Chapter 4, The Total Costs of Risk. It is estimated that at least 70% of these costs are hidden to the normal eye. So the costs seen of an incident in reality only are 30% of the actual costs. This is why it is so important to lower the number of at risk moments.

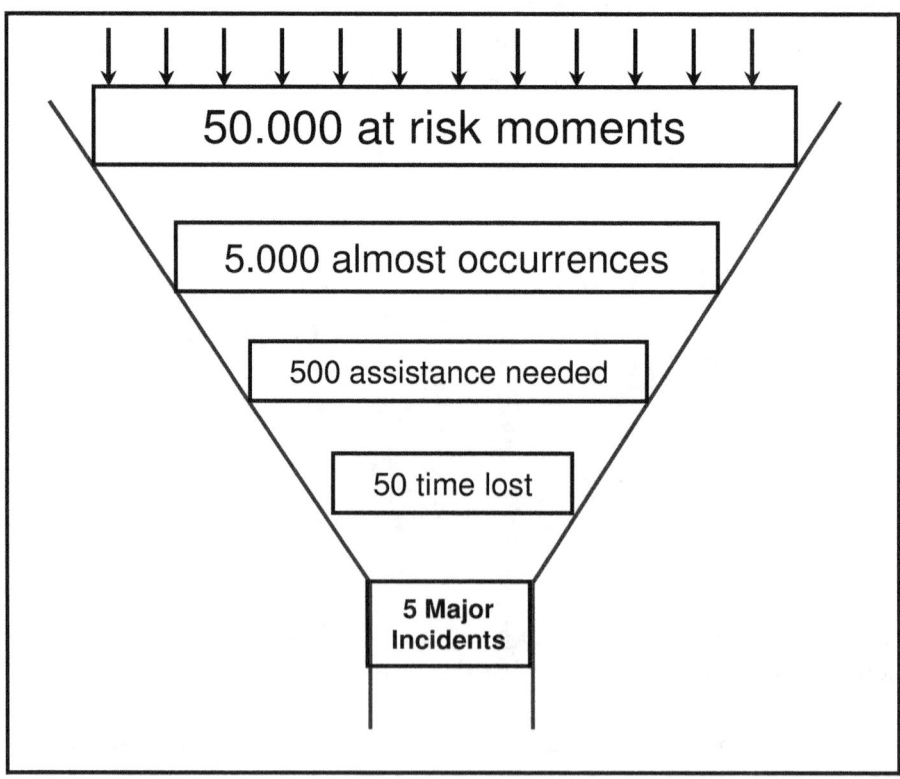

3 DIVIDING RISKS

How do we divide risks; well many methods exists, I just want to show you some of the more important ones in my view.

Risk caused by internal versus external factors.
Some risks are internal; companies have (limited) control over them. Others are external and cannot be influenced.

Manageable versus unmanageable risks.
Careful precautions can eliminate many risks, but some cannot be eliminated by any kind of risk management.

Extraordinary versus recurrent risks.
Most business risk insurance covers extraordinary one-off risks, rather than recurrent risks.

These divisions show where the risks come from, now to be able to make any decision on handling risks, first let us have a look at where we place the risks:

In principle we have three groups of risks;
Bottom-layer risks.
Middle-layer risks.
Top-layer risks.

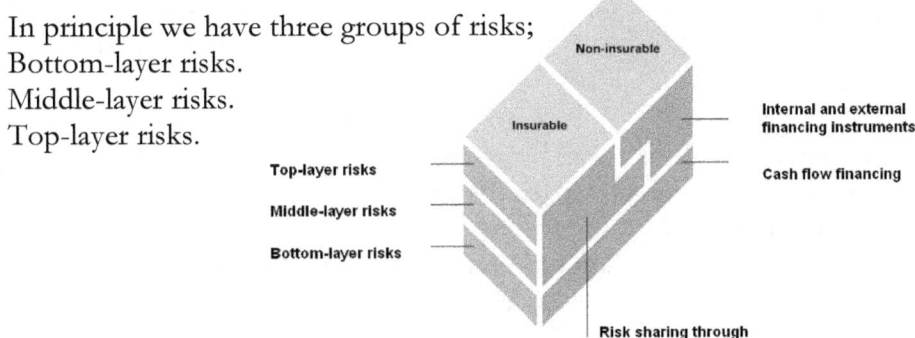

Risks in the bottom layer are typically high in frequency and low in severity. Examples include auto fleet insurance, most marine coverage and some types of property risk. Claims costs for this layer are often referred to as "burning costs", as the total sum of them is highly predictable for any corporation on an annual basis and the premium is therefore "burned" / used-up every year.

Through risk transference and self insuring schemes, this layer can be mainly "handled" effectively.

In the middle layer claims are moderate in frequency and severity and the cost of risk in this layer can be predicted over a five- to ten-year horizon.

Fire, liability and engineering coverage typically fall into this category.

Corporate customers with risks in this layer will have to focus not only on the price of the insurance, but mainly on an insurers capability to structure coverage and on its reputation in claims-handling.

Here, risk financing solutions can be sought; one must learn to manage the trade-off between self-insurance which is almost obligatory in the bottom layer and part traditional cover in the middle layer.

In the top layer we find those claims which are hard to measure and predict, especially in liability.

Typical exposures are in product and environmental liability, catastrophic property damage and business interruption.

Unlike the bottom and middle layer, here we need to use a clear risk transfer method.

Many corporations in Europe are not yet fully aware of the extent and breadth of their catastrophic exposure. It is therefore imperative that corporate customers choose carriers for their strength, size and relevant risk know-how and closely cooperate with their insurance and risk advisors.

Of course, not all risks can be insured or need to be insured; the small frequency-type of loss can be handled on a cash-flow basis, and so minimize the costs.

The catastrophic risks should be financed with the idea of obtaining a maximum security.

Bob Kruijsse at a Risk Management presentation in 2009.

Bob Kruijsse

4 TOTAL COSTS OF RISK

Are you paying too much for your Risk Financing? Look at your Total Costs of Risk.

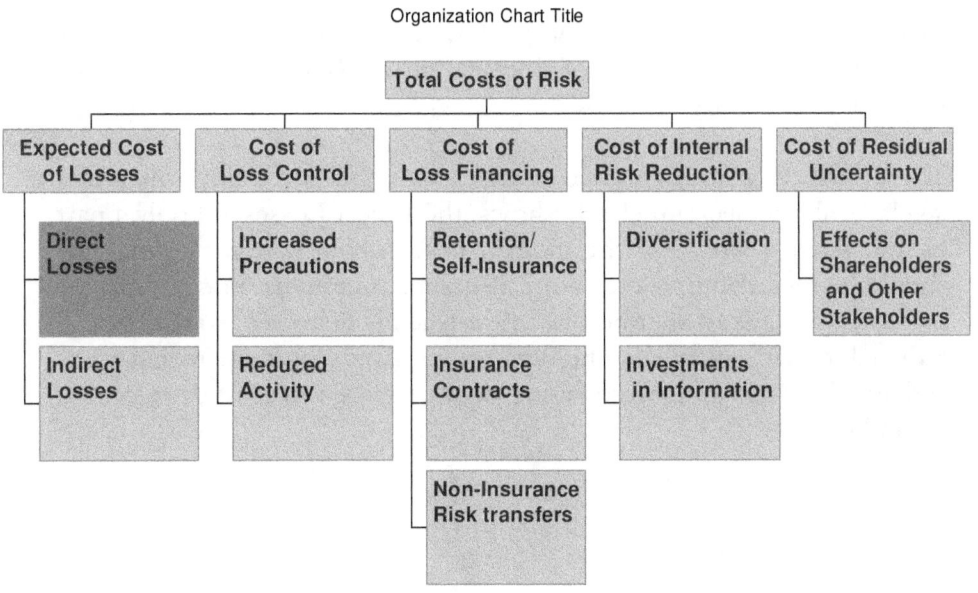

Organization Chart Title

What are the Total Costs of Risk?

TCoR (Total Costs of Risk) is a standard way to calculate your real costs of insurance and risk management efforts.

In basics, calculating your Total Costs of Risk is simple:

First add up all your insurance premiums. These will be your automobile, liability, property, crime, directors and officers, errors and omissions, aviation, cargo etc., depending on your organization. Secondly you add up all the costs you have had following an occurrence, which were not paid by your insurer. These will be deductibles, but also other costs not paid out. Then the expenses paid to your insurance intermediary directly (if you have any).
After this you get all the costs of handling your insurances inside of the organization.
Those are just the directly seeable costs, but it will give you the beginning of an outline.

In short: Costs of loss Financing + Expected Costs of Losses + Costs of Loss Control + Costs of Internal Loss Reduction + Costs of Residual Uncertainty = TCoR.

These include all the "hidden costs", costs that are below the water level. As above diagram clearly shows, the Direct Losses are only a part of any actual claim. All the indirect costs which you get or may get should be included in these. Your insurance premiums may go up after a claim; you have to wait before a new truck is delivered, so you have a reduced activity; your shareholders are unhappy, because to have less activity. This may cause a lowering of your share-price. And we can go on and on.

5 INFORMATION

Information is the most expensive and difficult to obtain commodity in the Risk Management process, as Peter Bernstein in his book *"Against the Gods" - The remarkable story of Risk* already clearly stated.

You never have enough information and if you have information, it is never adequate to your needs. Also, it is mainly quite expensive to obtain the information you need in order to be able to proceed with a good Risk Management Process.

Information is required in every step taken during the Risk Management Process. From the first analysis until the final decision on how to proceed once a certain risk has actually appeared.

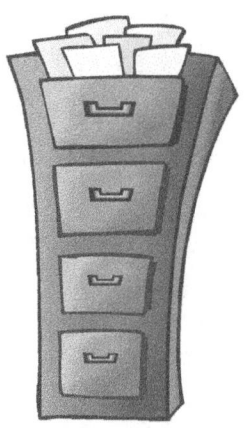

Information must be (made) available in a useable form for the Risk Management Analyst. This may mean by allowing the RMA to question personnel in an organization, to allow access to all documentation concerning historical and current risk and insurance data and by full support of the Board of an organization.

A Risk Management Analysis, as described in the next chapter, cannot work without full disclosure and cooperation by the Board of an organization.

6 RISK MANAGEMENT ANALYSIS

Here I would like to go deeper into the actual system of Risk Management Analysis. In this chapter I will introduce you to my Risk Management Analysis Program, its backgrounds, questionnaires and reasoning's. It is a system I have used on many occasions in order to analyze the risks of an organization and to decide how to proceed in handling them.

Risk Management Analysis can give an organization the solution, which they have been looking for and which final goal is the reducing to an acceptable level of those risks, which up to now were unacceptable.

In order to be able to proceed with such program the person(s) providing this need to have full support on a very high (board) level of the organization, so that it will ensure that everyone in the organization will cooperate.

At this moment, an internal coordinator is appointed, who will be the liaison between all parties interested. For this Coordinator, we prepare an introduction with a special list of questions (Attachment nr. 1), which we later use in the main questionnaires and which gives the Risk Management Analyst background information on the working of the organization.

Now we must identify which risks we run and create a list of risks to start the whole exercise with. That is done by research; conducting interviews with many people in an organization and finally, based upon that a list, an initial risk inventory, can be created.

The risk inventory is then put into a Risk Matrix (see attachment nr. 2), together with known, existing basic risks.

This is done in Phase I of the Risk Management Analysis Program, during which we also have extensive discussions in the organization to be analyzed with people working in different parts of said organization. This will allow for an extensive overview of how the organization works and what responsibilities lay where.

In Phase II we start the ranking of risks, based upon identified risks. Now, jointly with the sponsoring member of the management board, the scoring of Severity (see table on page 23) is to be agreed.

This severity is something which is different for each organization depending on their risk appetite. For a huge corporation, 10.000 Euro is not too much, but for a small, local company, this may already be a major financial impact.

Now we start making the questionnaires, based upon general questions, organization specific questions and some additional questions as requested by the Management Board. After this, they are ready to be sent, together with a letter from the Board, to the chosen participants from every department in the organization, so to get a good cross-referenced set of information.
The questionnaires (see an example in attachment 4) are based upon the risk matrix plus additional information retrieved during Phase I. With the questionnaire itself, we give an introduction to the participant (Attachment No. 2)

Once the questionnaires have been returned, the real analysis work starts. Here is where the knowledge and the experience of the Risk Management Specialist is required. This RMS must analyze all the questionnaires and put the results into a preliminary Risk Map (Attachment No. 5). The total score following individual scores for Probability, Development and Severity are calculated as follows: (Probability+Development)xSeverity=Total Score.

Probability

1	Extremely rare	Once every 100 years
2	Occurs rarely	Once every 10-25 tears
3	Occurs periodically	Once every 3-5 years
4	Occurs regularly	Once per year
5	Occurs with sufficient regularity to be accurately estimable	Multiple times per year

Development

0	Development is not a factor	N/A
1	Develops over a long period of time providing opportunity to	Months or years of warning (eg legislative changes)
2	Develops quickly, but impact is recurring in	Hours or days of warning (eg Product Recall)
3	Occurs suddenly - Impact is	No warning (eg. system crash)

Severity

1	Small loss	< 10.000
2	Large loss but not material	> 100.000
3	Minimum level of financial materiality	> 1.000.000
4	Major financial impact	> 10.000.000
5	Potential to imperil organization's strategy/ market perception	> 25.000.000

With the Risk Map and the preliminary scores of the analysis, a Brainstorm Session is started, with participation of all, who filled out a questionnaire.

Such a session may take between 4 and 8 hours, depending on the complexity of the matter.

During this session, the average results of the analysis will be discussed by all Participants and a final score will be agreed upon for each and every risk.

Not only does this Brainstorm give us the answers we may have been looking for, it also gives the different departments in the organization an understanding of the problems other departments struggle with and the risks involved in them. Participants will state that they, for the first time, understand what other parts of the organizations have as risks and what these are all about.

Once again the Risk Management Specialist will go over all the answers and put the results in a Risk Ranking list and Risk Map *(see attachment 5)*, which will now clearly show, which risks are the most important for the organization.

But this is not all. Now the analyst will start to look at the interconnection between certain possible risks; e.g. a Fire damage to a building may also cause a Business Interruption loss. And there will be many more likewise. This is all done in Phase III.

Once this list has been exhausted, recommendations for what to do with certain risks may follow, as well as an analysis of the current insurance program and its adequateness to the risks discovered.

In Phase IV we start looking at solutions to the final list of Risks. The insurance program may need changes, as well as the current security program in place in the organization. This requires a close cooperation between Insurance, Legal and Security together with Operations.

Now finally we can say that we are starting to have a Risk Management System in place in our organization; one that does the work required of it and is not a "dead" document lying somewhere on a shelf or deeply buried in a file cabinet.

Phase I Risk Identification

Objective: Create a comprehensive list of potential risks

Actions: 1.   Gathering of relevant operational, financial and
                strategic information;
         2.   Conduct interviews with key staff;
         3.   Creating initial risk inventory.

Phase II Risk Ranking

Objective: Apply Scoring System to risks identified in Phase I
               in order to prioritize risks.

Actions: 1.   Agree on scoring dimensions for Probability,
                Severity and Development;
         2.   Questionnaires are prepared for 8 or 9 Participants;
         3.   Analysis of questionnaires;
         4.   Development of preliminary scores based upon
                questionnaires and preparing of first Risk Map*;
         5.   Brainstorm Session;
         6.   A list of "Priority" risks is created;

Phase III: Data Collection & Modeling

Objective: Utilize relevant internal and external data to define
               the dimensions of priority risks.
Actions: 1.   Develop loss distributions for individual risks based
                on loss statistics provided;
         2.   Analyze potential risk portfolios;
         3.   Conduct catastrophic risk simulations based upon
                PML or EML;
         4.   Analysis of existing insurance portfolio

Phase IV: Solutions

Objective: Use risk information to determine the optimal risk mitigation and financing strategies.

Actions: 1.   Run Financial Analysis to test various risk financing strategies under different loss scenarios;
2.   Evaluate realistic alternatives given data quality;
3.   Setup a Risk Management System,
4.   Approach and discuss with risk partners, as needed;
5.   Providing Risk Management System during the year, including but not limited to risk-handling (incl. insurance and non-insurance claims)
6.   Checking of Third Parties Tenant's Liability policies (including renewal checks);
7.   Half yearly meetings with the board to discuss current Risk Management Issues (or more often if required).

* *Risk mapping is a technique used to view identified risks and decide what risk mitigation method would be best to use on that risk. It is a simple, but very powerful tool. See an example Risk Map in Attachment 5.*

7 RISK REGISTER

Once we have all those risks analyzed and we know what (may) happen to us, we will have to get a Risk Register in place, in which we do not only have all the risks found during our exercise, but which is a living database, in which all risks are registered and all occurrences are analyzed on their how and what.

This will allow for a continuing Risk Management System, handled by a competent Risk Manager in close cooperation with the members of the Risk Management Committee. By setting up a formal Risk Management Committee within the organization, including in it participants from all parts of the organization, individuals at all levels will be galvanized to include consideration and control of risk in their daily planning and decision making.

The Risk Manager is the Executive of the Risk Management Committee and prepares his reporting after consultation with the committee for the Board.

The Risk Manager's role is **NOT** the having of the technical knowledge of the organization he/she is working for and does the analyzing and risk management for, but his/her role is having the knowledge of how to combine the knowledge already in place in the existing (e.g. technical) staff of the organization and compile this into a working Risk Management Process.

The aim of a risk management approach is not to make the Organization risk-averse, but to effectively identify, assess, treat and monitor the risks at a strategic and operational level.

The Risk Register as shown below, is a living organism, which continuously flows with the organization according to the needs of the Risk Management and should be dynamic, and must reflect the current status of risks and risk actions. Risk management activities and risk information must move ahead together.

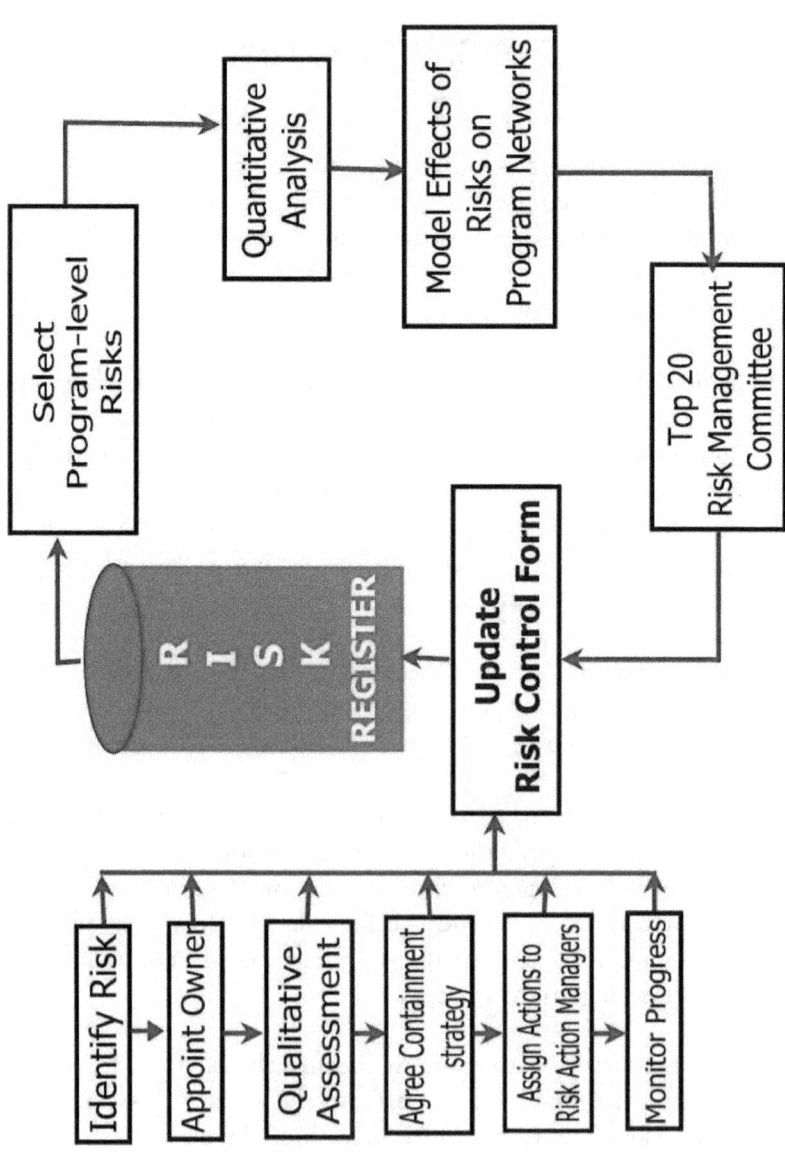

8 RISK MANAGEMENT ORGANIZATION

The Risk Management Organization includes the following:

The **Risk Management Committee** includes participants from all part levels of the organization and assists the Risk Manager in risk management activities. They regularly review risks that could potentially have the most significant impact on the program (the "Top Twenty" risks). The jointly agree upon the list of Risk Owners.

The **Risk Owners** are selected by the risk manager and/or the risk management committee. They are responsible for formulating and implementing risk containment strategies. Risk owners are normally the managers most likely to be affected by the occurrence of the risks concerned.

Risk Action Managers are assigned by risk owners, and handle specific actions within the risk management strategy, as agreed upon with the Risk Manager.

ATTACHMENT 1
Discussion with Coordinator

Here are the questions that we would like to discuss with you regarding your organization's risk management best practices.

1. Overview and context for risk management

1. How does your organization define risk in the context of its business or environment?
2. Does your organization have a general risk management objective which guides risk management activities?
3. Do the objectives and values of managing risk represent a new way of doing business in your organization?
4. What are the benefits of managing risk for your organization?
   (Consider: communication for commitment; enhancement of stakeholder value or achievement of objectives; measurement for improved management; support for accountability and governance; strengthening of the planning and decision-making process (such as communication or synergy); increased confidence of stakeholders; measurable returns on investments).

2. Integrating risk management into the management practices of your organization

Are there some best practices or lessons learned (obstacles overcome) that you would like to tell us about, or any other practice for integration.

1. Can you describe in general terms how your organization defines the objectives and values for managing risk and communicates them in the organization?
2. Does your organization have a formal risk management policy?
3. What are the key features/messages conveyed? (*Consider:*

    - *Objectives/principles*
    - *Opportunity and risk taking*
    - *Risk coverage*
    - *Risk tolerances and risk limits*
    - *A supportive work environment (i.e. Tolerance for mistakes)*
    - *Integrating risk management with other management processes)*

4. How are risk tolerances established and managed (i.e. at the corporate or local level)?
5. Can you describe in general terms how your organization reflects shared responsibility for managing risks and fostering commitment in your organization's governance and administrative bodies?
6. What responsibilities do governing bodies of your organization (e.g., Board of Directors, Senior Management Committees, etc.) and senior management have for managing risks? Are they held accountable? If so, how?
7. How does the responsibility/accountability for managing risks flow through the organization (e.g., through management/administration levels, to all employees)? How are people held accountable?
8. Are significant risks communicated to stakeholders? If so, how often, and in what context? Who communicates these to the stakeholders?

9. a) Can you describe in general terms how your organization identifies and evaluates organization-wide risks?

b) Once the risks are identified, how does this information support the management process (planning, resource allocation and decision-making)?

10. What techniques and methods are used for identifying and evaluating risks? (Consider:

- *The types of risks*
- *How risks are identified*
- *How risks are quantified*
- *How risks are prioritized)*

11. Are the techniques and methods easily understood and used by managers? *(Consider: use of plain language and user-friendliness).*

12. Are the results of the evaluation integrated into existing management processes (e.g., planning, resource allocation and decision-making)? How?

13. Does the evaluation consider stakeholders' view of risk and the opportunity costs of a risk that is not taken?

14. To what extent has risk management supported change and cultural shifts in your organization?

15. Can you describe in general terms how your organization manages or reduces risk through an internal system of control and other strategies?

16. Have your strategies or processes for managing risks been changing? In what way?

17. Are stakeholders, customers, suppliers or other external bodies involved in your risk management process? In what way?

18. Can you describe in general terms how your organization monitors the process of managing risks and communicates and reports on this to

senior management, the governing body and key stakeholders?

19. Is the success in achieving risk management objectives monitored and measured?
20. Does your organization use a specific structure/medium to report on risk management?
21. What is the role of internal audit in your risk management program? *(Consider: monitoring compliance; compliance and providing best practices improvement or advice, best practices, methods, etc.)*

3. Implementing risk management in your organization

Are there some best practices or lessons learned (obstacles overcome) that you would like to relate to us, or any other practice for implementation? Do you have examples of tools that should not be used?

1. Can you describe in general terms how your organization implements risk management?
2. Have any tools been particularly effective? Why?

4. Disciplines and functions that manage risks

1. Are there disciplines and functions within your organization which manage risks at an operational level? Which ones?
2. Are there best practices/lessons learned (obstacles overcome) associated with the management process used to initiate and implement risk management in this/these disciplines and functions?

3. Are there any documents that you can provide to us to help us understand your risk management practices?
4. Can we call you again if we need to clarify or elaborate on your responses?
5. Are there any articles or publications that you found particularly useful in your risk management activities? (List)

ATTACHMENT 2
Example Basic Risk Matrix

Financial Risks	Labour Risks	Liability Risks	Natural Risks
1.1 Extortion	2.1 Illness	3.1 Contracts	4.1 Earthquake
1.2 Impoundment	2.2 Accident	3.2 Production, Services	4.2 Ice Storm
1.3 Credit Risks	2.3 Kidnapping	3.3 Profession	4.3 Flood
1.4 Subsidy risk	2.4 Strikes	3.4 Directors and Officers	4.4 Wind Storm (Hurricane)
1.5 (contracts)	2.5 Espionage, Knowledge	3.5 Employees	4.5 Lightning
1.6 Foreign Exchange	2.6 Employment Practices	3.6 Motor vehicles	4.6 Tornado
1.7 Interest Rate Risk	2.7 Labor Disputes	3.7 Assets in care, custody or control	4.7 Seasonal Abnormality
1.8 Inventory Valuation	2.8 Workplace Violence	3.8 Advertising Liability	
1.9 Acquisition Liabilities	2.9 Employee recruitment retention	3.9 Internet Liability	
1.10 Disputes	2.10 Workers' Compensation Disability	3.10 Intellectual Property	
1.11 Punitive Damages		3.11 Marine Liability	
1.12		3.12 Aircraft Liability	
		3.13 Environmental Risk	
		3.14 Emission into the earth	
		3.15	
		3.16	
		3.17	
		3.18	
		3.19	
		3.20	
The Financial position will be directly affected following financial losses	The Labour capacity will be affected as well as abstenteeism and quality of labour	The Financial position will be affected through claims by third parties following legal or contractual liability	Damage or loss of buildings, installations, inventory, transportation equipment and goods. The production capacity will be affected through partial or complete standstill of the company

Operational Risks		Political Risks		Technological Risks	
5.1	Theft and burglary	6.1	Antitrust	7.1	Internet
5.2	Machinery Damage	6.2	Local Zoning Disputes	7.2	Computer virus
5.3	Collapsing of buildings	6.3	Confiscation/Nationalization	7.3	Computer Hacker
5.4	Fire, Explosion	6.4	Trade Disruption	7.4	Data Center Malfunction (not
5.5	Water, Oil, Smoke, Soot	6.5	Third World Manufacturing	7.5	Computer failure
5.6	Falling Objects	6.6	Sabotage, Destruction	7.6	Computer system installation project
5.7	Transport incidents				
5.8	Business Interruption				
5.9	Consequential Damage				
5.10	Failure of energy				
5.11	Supplier Failure to Deliver				
5.12	Loss of data, drawings				
5.13	Product Pollution				
5.14	Product Contamination				
5.15	Product Uncorrect prescriptions,				
5.16	Product Poisoning				
5.17	Product Uncorrect usage, uncorrect				
5.18	Failure of transport availability				
5.19	No raw materials				
5.20	Wrong specification of materials				
5.21	Statical Electricity, Short circuitry				
Damage or loss of buildings, installations, inventory, transportation equipment and goods. The production capacity will be affected through partial or complete standstill of the company		The Sales or production facilities will no longer be available		The technology used is rendered unusable following an event inside the technology itself	

ATTACHMENT 3
Introduction for Participants

Introduction to the participants – the forthcoming exercise

As you know, we will shortly be undertaking an exercise the objectives of which are to:

- Assist in the process of identifying risks that could threaten our Organization.
- Collectively agree the relative priority of each risk.
- Create a map that demonstrates the relationship between threats, assets and goals.
- Establish some clarity around the top killer scenarios.

Our Risk Management Consultant, who has considerable experience of this type of process, will assist us in the exercise. His role will be that of catalyst and mediator, but it is our process, fuelled by our knowledge of our business and its trading dynamics.

The core of the process is a structured "brainstorm", based on our subjective scoring of the significance of the risks and issues that are contained within the risk model incorporated into this pack.

The brainstorm itself will consist of the following stages:

1. A debate on the risk model. Significant differences in the scores that you have each given for our corporate goals, business assets and risks will be debated and the scores adjusted as necessary. (The objective being to flush out issues not achieve uniform scores!).

2. Selecting the top risks contained within the risk model by using an agreed cut-off point against the collective scores for each – typically, the top 10% of the <180 risks within the model would be selected. These will then be the focus of the remainder of the session.

3. An open discussion, in which
The key threats will be developed
Who how and when should take what possible action

The purpose of this pack is to:

Help you prepare for the exercise by capturing your immediate assessment of some of the issues involved.
Record your subjective scoring of our goals, key business drivers and most significant risks. These can be combined prior to the brainstorm and, after a debate on areas of significant difference, used to build our risk model.

Therefore please complete the check boxes in the rest of the pack, and return them to me for collation the next day.

Please allow c. 45 minutes of quality time to complete the pack. You should pace yourself not spend any more than that.

During the Brainstorm session we will discuss the main threats to the organization. Please think about the following risks in this context and score them. If, according to you, a certain risk does not exist in your organization, do not fill out anything.

Definitions

Probability   How regularly does the risk event occur?

Development   Can you foresee the occurrence?

Severity   How large could the resulting loss be and how important is that to our organization?

WE ARE NOW ASKING YOU TO USE A DIFFERENT BASIS OF MEASUREMENT.

Identify and evaluate the threat scenarios

During the brainstorm we will consider the threats to the high scored goals and assets above. Please consider the following threats within that context, and score them to reflect your view of the significance of the threat.

Please add additional risks/threats as YOU see them.

ATTACHMENT 4
Questionnaire

Financial Risks

The position of the organization may be touched directly following such occurrence:

		Probability					Development				Severity				
		1	2	3	4	5	3	2	1	0	1	2	3	4	5
1.1	Extortion	◻	◻	◻	◻	◻	◻	◻	◻	◻	◻	◻	◻	◻	◻
1.2	Impoundment	◻	◻	◻	◻	◻	◻	◻	◻	◻	◻	◻	◻	◻	◻
1.3	Credit Risks	◻	◻	◻	◻	◻	◻	◻	◻	◻	◻	◻	◻	◻	◻
1.4	Subsidy risk	◻	◻	◻	◻	◻	◻	◻	◻	◻	◻	◻	◻	◻	◻
1.5	Trade incompetence (mistakes in contracts)	◻	◻	◻	◻	◻	◻	◻	◻	◻	◻	◻	◻	◻	◻
1.6	Foreign Exchange	◻	◻	◻	◻	◻	◻	◻	◻	◻	◻	◻	◻	◻	◻
1.7	Interest Rate Risk	◻	◻	◻	◻	◻	◻	◻	◻	◻	◻	◻	◻	◻	◻
1.8	Inventory Valuation	◻	◻	◻	◻	◻	◻	◻	◻	◻	◻	◻	◻	◻	◻
1.9	Acquisition Liabilities	◻	◻	◻	◻	◻	◻	◻	◻	◻	◻	◻	◻	◻	◻
1.10	Disputes	◻	◻	◻	◻	◻	◻	◻	◻	◻	◻	◻	◻	◻	◻
1.11	Punitive Damages	◻	◻	◻	◻	◻	◻	◻	◻	◻	◻	◻	◻	◻	◻
1.12	Extortion	◻	◻	◻	◻	◻	◻	◻	◻	◻	◻	◻	◻	◻	◻
1.13	Impoundment	◻	◻	◻	◻	◻	◻	◻	◻	◻	◻	◻	◻	◻	◻
1.14	Credit Risks	◻	◻	◻	◻	◻	◻	◻	◻	◻	◻	◻	◻	◻	◻
1.15	Subsidy risk	◻	◻	◻	◻	◻	◻	◻	◻	◻	◻	◻	◻	◻	◻
		Extremely Rare	Occurs rarely	Occurs periodically	Occurs regularly	Occurs with sufficient regularity	Occurs totally unforeseen	Develops fast, but ...	Develops long and gives enough time ...	Almost certain	Small claim	Average claim, but unimportant	Average claim with real financial consequences	Large claim with huge financial ...	Claim which may cripple company financially

Labour Risks

The position of the organization may be touched directly following such occurrence:

		Probability					Development				Severity				
		1	2	3	4	5	3	2	1	0	1	2	3	4	5
2.1	Ilness	△	△	△	△	△	△	△	△	△	△	△	△	△	△
2.2	Accident	△	△	△	△	△	△	△	△	△	△	△	△	△	△
2.3	Kidnapping	△	△	△	△	△	△	△	△	△	△	△	△	△	△
2.4	Strikes	△	△	△	△	△	△	△	△	△	△	△	△	△	△
2.5	Espionage, Knowledge	△	△	△	△	△	△	△	△	△	△	△	△	△	△
2.6	Employment Practices	△	△	△	△	△	△	△	△	△	△	△	△	△	△
2.7	Labor Disputes	△	△	△	△	△	△	△	△	△	△	△	△	△	△
2.8	Workplace Violence	△	△	△	△	△	△	△	△	△	△	△	△	△	△
2.9	Employee recruitment retention	△	△	△	△	△	△	△	△	△	△	△	△	△	△
2.10	Workers' Compensation Disability	△	△	△	△	△	△	△	△	△	△	△	△	△	△
2.11		△	△	△	△	△	△	△	△	△	△	△	△	△	△
2.12		△	△	△	△	△	△	△	△	△	△	△	△	△	△
2.13		△	△	△	△	△	△	△	△	△	△	△	△	△	△
		Extremely Rare	Occurs rarely	Occurs periodically	Occurs regularly	Occurs with sufficient regularity	Occurs really unforeseen	Develops fast, but....	Develops long and gives enough time....	Almost certain	Small claim	Average claim, but unimportant	Average claim with real financial consequences	Large claim with huge financial....	Claim which may cripple company financially

Liability Risks

The position of the organization may be touched directly following an occurrence of a third-party claim:

		Probability						Development				Severity				
		1	2	3	4	5	3	2	1	0	1	2	3	4	5
3.1	Contracts	△	△	△	△	△	△	△	△	△	△	△	△	△	△
3.2	Production, Services	△	△	△	△	△	△	△	△	△	△	△	△	△	△
3.3	Profession	△	△	△	△	△	△	△	△	△	△	△	△	△	△
3.4	Directors and Officers	△	△	△	△	△	△	△	△	△	△	△	△	△	△
3.5	Employees	△	△	△	△	△	△	△	△	△	△	△	△	△	△
3.6	Motor vehicles	△	△	△	△	△	△	△	△	△	△	△	△	△	△
3.7	Assets in care, custody or control	△	△	△	△	△	△	△	△	△	△	△	△	△	△
3.8	Advertising Liability	△	△	△	△	△	△	△	△	△	△	△	△	△	△
3.9	Internet Liability	△	△	△	△	△	△	△	△	△	△	△	△	△	△
3.10	Intellectual Property	△	△	△	△	△	△	△	△	△	△	△	△	△	△
3.11	Marine Liability	△	△	△	△	△	△	△	△	△	△	△	△	△	△
3.12	Aircraft Liability	△	△	△	△	△	△	△	△	△	△	△	△	△	△
3.13	Environmental Risk	△	△	△	△	△	△	△	△	△	△	△	△	△	△
3.14	Emission into the earth	△	△	△	△	△	△	△	△	△	△	△	△	△	△
3.15	Emission into the open water	△	△	△	△	△	△	△	△	△	△	△	△	△	△
3.16	Emission into the air	△	△	△	△	△	△	△	△	△	△	△	△	△	△
3.17	Wrong treatments (eg Chemical wastes)	△	△	△	△	△	△	△	△	△	△	△	△	△	△
3.18	Pollution of the groundwaters	△	△	△	△	△	△	△	△	△	△	△	△	△	△
3.19	Emission nuclear matter	△	△	△	△	△	△	△	△	△	△	△	△	△	△
3.20	Danger of radiation	△	△	△	△	△	△	△	△	△	△	△	△	△	△
		Extremely Rare	Occurs rarely	Occurs periodically	Occurs regularly	Occurs with sufficient regularity	Occurs totally unforeseen	Develops fast, but...	Develops long and gives enough time...	Almost certain	Small claim	Average claim, but unimportant	Average claim with real financial consequences	Large claim with huge financial ...	Claim which may cripple company financially

Natural Risks

The position of the organization may be touched directly following such occurrence against property etc.:

		Probability					Development				Severity				
		1	2	3	4	5	3	2	1	0	1	2	3	4	5
4.1	Earthquake	△	△	△	△	△	△	△	△	△	△	△	△	△	△
4.2	Ice Storm	△	△	△	△	△	△	△	△	△	△	△	△	△	△
4.3	Flood	△	△	△	△	△	△	△	△	△	△	△	△	△	△
4.4	Wind Storm (Hurricane)	△	△	△	△	△	△	△	△	△	△	△	△	△	△
4.5	Lightning	△	△	△	△	△	△	△	△	△	△	△	△	△	△
4.6	Tornado	△	△	△	△	△	△	△	△	△	△	△	△	△	△
4.7	Seasonal Abnormality	△	△	△	△	△	△	△	△	△	△	△	△	△	△
4.8		△	△	△	△	△	△	△	△	△	△	△	△	△	△
4.9		△	△	△	△	△	△	△	△	△	△	△	△	△	△

Probability scale:
1 Extremely Rare
2 Occurs rarely
3 Occurs periodically
4 Occurs regularly
5 Occurs with sufficient regularity

Development scale:
3 Occurs totally unforeseen
2 Develops fast, but....
1 Develops long and gives enough time....
0 Almost certain

Severity scale:
1 Small claim
2 Average claim, but unimportant
3 Average claim with real financial consequences
4 Large claim with huge financial....
5 Claim which may cripple company financially

Operational Risks

The position of the organization may be touched directly following such occurrence:

		Probability					Development				Severity				
		1	2	3	4	5	3	2	1	0	1	2	3	4	5
5.1	Fire, Explosion	△	△	△	△	△	△	△	△	△	△	△	△	△	△
5.2	Water, Oil, Smoke, Soot	△	△	△	△	△	△	△	△	△	△	△	△	△	△
5.3	Falling Objects	△	△	△	△	△	△	△	△	△	△	△	△	△	△
5.4	Transport incidents	△	△	△	△	△	△	△	△	△	△	△	△	△	△
5.5	Business Interruption	△	△	△	△	△	△	△	△	△	△	△	△	△	△
5.6	Consequential Damage	△	△	△	△	△	△	△	△	△	△	△	△	△	△
5.7	Failure of energy	△	△	△	△	△	△	△	△	△	△	△	△	△	△
5.8	Supplier Failure to Deliver	△	△	△	△	△	△	△	△	△	△	△	△	△	△
5.9	Loss of data, drawings	△	△	△	△	△	△	△	△	△	△	△	△	△	△
5.10	Product Pollution	△	△	△	△	△	△	△	△	△	△	△	△	△	△
5.11	Product Contamination	△	△	△	△	△	△	△	△	△	△	△	△	△	△
5.12	Product Uncorrect prescriptions, packaging	△	△	△	△	△	△	△	△	△	△	△	△	△	△
5.13	Product Poisoning	△	△	△	△	△	△	△	△	△	△	△	△	△	△
5.14	Fire, Explosion	△	△	△	△	△	△	△	△	△	△	△	△	△	△
5.15	Water, Oil, Smoke, Soot	△	△	△	△	△	△	△	△	△	△	△	△	△	△
5.16	Falling Objects	△	△	△	△	△	△	△	△	△	△	△	△	△	△
5.17	Product Uncorrect usage, uncorrect advise	△	△	△	△	△	△	△	△	△	△	△	△	△	△
5.18	Failure of transport availability	△	△	△	△	△	△	△	△	△	△	△	△	△	△
5.19	No raw materials	△	△	△	△	△	△	△	△	△	△	△	△	△	△
5.20	Wrong specification of materials	△	△	△	△	△	△	△	△	△	△	△	△	△	△
		Extremely Rare	Occurs rarely	Occurs periodically	Occurs regularly	Occurs with sufficient regularity	Occurs totally unforeseen	Develops fast, but...	Develops long and gives enough time...	Almost certain	Small claim	Average claim, but unimportant	Average claim with real financial consequences	Large claim with huge financial...	Claim which may cripple company financially

Political Risks

The position of the organization or its functioning may be touched directly following such occurrence:

	Probability					Development				Severity				
	1	2	3	4	5	3	2	1	0	1	2	3	4	5
6.1 Antitrust	△	△	△	△	△	△	△	△	△	△	△	△	△	△
6.2 Local Zoning Disputes	△	△	△	△	△	△	△	△	△	△	△	△	△	△
6.3 Confiscation/Nationalization	△	△	△	△	△	△	△	△	△	△	△	△	△	△
6.4 Trade Disruption	△	△	△	△	△	△	△	△	△	△	△	△	△	△
6.5 Thirld World Manufacturing	△	△	△	△	△	△	△	△	△	△	△	△	△	△
6.6 Sabotage, Destruction	△	△	△	△	△	△	△	△	△	△	△	△	△	△
6.7	△	△	△	△	△	△	△	△	△	△	△	△	△	△
6.8	△	△	△	△	△	△	△	△	△	△	△	△	△	△
6.9	△	△	△	△	△	△	△	△	△	△	△	△	△	△
6.10	△	△	△	△	△	△	△	△	△	△	△	△	△	△
	Extremely Rare	Occurs rarely	Occurs periodically	Occurs regularly	Occurs with sufficient regularity	Occurs totally unforeseen	Develops fast, but...	Develops long and gives enough time....	Almost certain	Small claim	Average claim, but unimportant	Average claim with real financial consequences	Large claim with huge financial....	Claim which may cripple company financially

45

Technological Risks

The position of the organization may be touched directly following such occurrence in the electronics of the organization:

		Probability					Development				Severity				
		1	2	3	4	5	3	2	1	0	1	2	3	4	5
7.1	Internet	△	△	△	△	△	△	△	△	△	△	△	△	△	△
7.2	Computer virus	△	△	△	△	△	△	△	△	△	△	△	△	△	△
7.3	Computer Hacker	△	△	△	△	△	△	△	△	△	△	△	△	△	△
7.4	Data Center Malfunction (not hazard related)	△	△	△	△	△	△	△	△	△	△	△	△	△	△
7.5	Computer failure	△	△	△	△	△	△	△	△	△	△	△	△	△	△
7.6	Computer system installation project failure	△	△	△	△	△	△	△	△	△	△	△	△	△	△
		Extremely Rare	Occurs rarely	Occurs periodically	Occurs regularly	Occurs with sufficient regularity	Occurs totally unforeseen	Develops fast, but....	Develops long and gives enough time....	Almost certain	Small claim	Average claim, but unimportant	Average claim with real financial consequences	Large claim with huge financial....	Claim which may cripple company financially

Other Risks YOU see

The position of the organization may be touched directly following an occurrence:

	Probability					Development				Severity				
	1	2	3	4	5	3	2	1	0	1	2	3	4	5
8.1	⌂	⌂	⌂	⌂	⌂	⌂	⌂	⌂	⌂	⌂	⌂	⌂	⌂	⌂
8.2	⌂	⌂	⌂	⌂	⌂	⌂	⌂	⌂	⌂	⌂	⌂	⌂	⌂	⌂
8.3	⌂	⌂	⌂	⌂	⌂	⌂	⌂	⌂	⌂	⌂	⌂	⌂	⌂	⌂
8.4	⌂	⌂	⌂	⌂	⌂	⌂	⌂	⌂	⌂	⌂	⌂	⌂	⌂	⌂
8.5	⌂	⌂	⌂	⌂	⌂	⌂	⌂	⌂	⌂	⌂	⌂	⌂	⌂	⌂
8.6	⌂	⌂	⌂	⌂	⌂	⌂	⌂	⌂	⌂	⌂	⌂	⌂	⌂	⌂
8.7	⌂	⌂	⌂	⌂	⌂	⌂	⌂	⌂	⌂	⌂	⌂	⌂	⌂	⌂
8.8	⌂	⌂	⌂	⌂	⌂	⌂	⌂	⌂	⌂	⌂	⌂	⌂	⌂	⌂
8.9	⌂	⌂	⌂	⌂	⌂	⌂	⌂	⌂	⌂	⌂	⌂	⌂	⌂	⌂
8.10	⌂	⌂	⌂	⌂	⌂	⌂	⌂	⌂	⌂	⌂	⌂	⌂	⌂	⌂
8.11	⌂	⌂	⌂	⌂	⌂	⌂	⌂	⌂	⌂	⌂	⌂	⌂	⌂	⌂
8.12	⌂	⌂	⌂	⌂	⌂	⌂	⌂	⌂	⌂	⌂	⌂	⌂	⌂	⌂
8.13	⌂	⌂	⌂	⌂	⌂	⌂	⌂	⌂	⌂	⌂	⌂	⌂	⌂	⌂
8.14	⌂	⌂	⌂	⌂	⌂	⌂	⌂	⌂	⌂	⌂	⌂	⌂	⌂	⌂
8.15	⌂	⌂	⌂	⌂	⌂	⌂	⌂	⌂	⌂	⌂	⌂	⌂	⌂	⌂
8.16	⌂	⌂	⌂	⌂	⌂	⌂	⌂	⌂	⌂	⌂	⌂	⌂	⌂	⌂
8.17	⌂	⌂	⌂	⌂	⌂	⌂	⌂	⌂	⌂	⌂	⌂	⌂	⌂	⌂
8.18	⌂	⌂	⌂	⌂	⌂	⌂	⌂	⌂	⌂	⌂	⌂	⌂	⌂	⌂
8.19	⌂	⌂	⌂	⌂	⌂	⌂	⌂	⌂	⌂	⌂	⌂	⌂	⌂	⌂
8.20	⌂	⌂	⌂	⌂	⌂	⌂	⌂	⌂	⌂	⌂	⌂	⌂	⌂	⌂

Probability:
- Extremely Rare
- Occurs rarely
- Occurs periodically
- Occurs regularly
- Occurs with sufficient regularity

Development:
- Occurs totally unforeseen
- Develops fast, but....
- Develops long and gives enough time....
- Almost certain

Severity:
- Small claim
- Average claim, but unimportant
- Average claim with real financial consequences
- Large claim with huge financial....
- Claim which may cripple company financially

ATTACHMENT 5
Risk Map

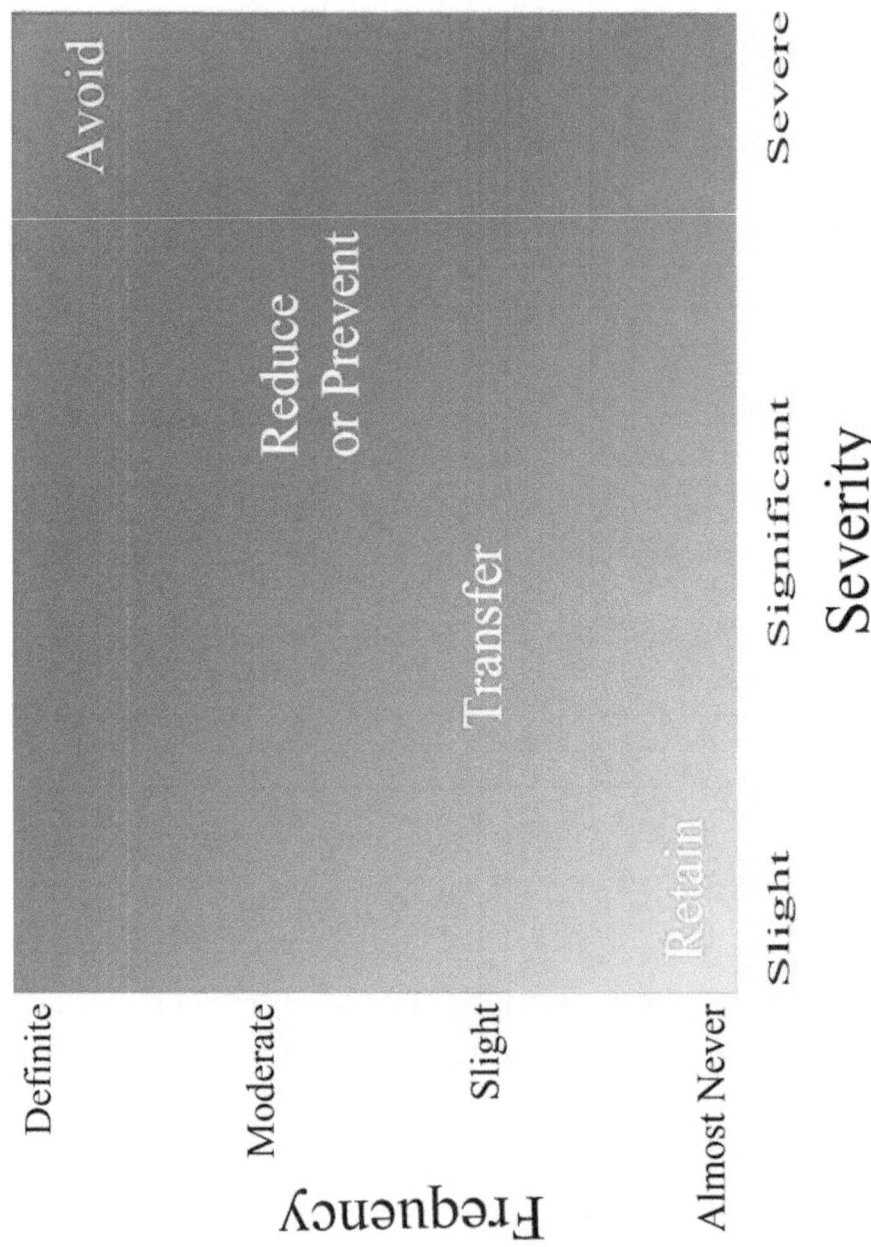

ABOUT THE AUTHOR

Bob Kruijsse is a Dutchman, who has been living in Poland now for over 22 years and has been in the Risk and Insurance business since 1980.

During this period he has worked as Risk and Insurance Manager, as Marine and General Insurance Broker, and as a Risk and Insurance Consultant/Manager.

He has extensive knowledge of Risk Management, having advised many types of corporations on risks and insurances throughout his career.

For almost 35 years now, he has studied the various aspects of risks and how to deal with them. Thanks to this kind of approach he has developed an instinctive feeling for risks and a very practical approach to risk management.

As a member of the Polish Association of Insurance and Reinsurance Brokers POLBROKERS he was responsible for drafting the Code of Ethics of this organization and chaired the Ethics Committee for many years.

He is one of the founding members of the Polish Association of Risk Management POLRISK.

He was also a founding member and Board member of the Dutch-Polish Chamber of Commerce, and has been chairman of the IGCC (International group of Chambers of Commerce in Poland).

Currently he is Insurance and Risk Manager for Central and Eastern Europe within the DHL Global Business Services organization and is located in Warsaw, Poland.

www.ingramcontent.com/pod-product-compliance
Lightning Source LLC
Chambersburg PA
CBHW071637170526
45166CB00003B/1348